W9-BYH-464

SOVEREIGN *of* TOMORROW

CONTENTS

PUBLICATIONS UK

This publication has been designed and published by Publications UK Ltd.
Tel: +44 (0) 20 8238 5000
Email: info@publicationsuk.co.uk
www.publicationsuk.co.uk

Managing Director: Stewart Lee
Editor: Thomas Corby MVO
Art Director: Hitesh Chauhan
Research & Production: Roshan Adam
Advertising: Ruth Levine

Picture Credits: The Press Association, Getty Images & The Royal Collection Trust

ISBN: 978-1-782-80112-2

© Publications UK LTD 2013. The Publishers make no recommendation in respect of any of the advertisers, and no recommendation may be implied by way of the presence of their advertisements.

A minimum of 20% from the net revenue received by the publisher from the sale price of this publication will be distributed between Help for Heroes Trading Limited which Gift Aids all of its taxable profits to Help for Heroes (Registered Charity Number 1120920) who will receive 12% and Bliss (Registered Charity Number 1002973) who will receive 8%.

The 2013 Hero Ride – riders cycle up the Mall in a Help for Heroes medal formation.

HRH The Duke of Cambridge meets a family at the opening of Tedworth House, a Help for Heroes run Recovery Centre in Wiltshire.

HRH Prince Harry meets the child of a wounded Serviceman at Help for Heroes Tedworth House.

FOREWORD

by Bryn and Emma Parry OBE, Help for Heroes Co-Founders

Help for Heroes was founded in 2007 by Bryn and Emma Parry and in just six years, with the support of the British public, has been instrumental in developing the provision of care to those suffering life-changing injury or illness as a result of their service. The Road to Recovery is a very long and hard path, but working with other Service charities and the Ministry of Defence, Help for Heroes aims to ensure that the journey is as smooth as possible.

Addressing a gathering which included volunteers, H4H staff, supporters and over 100 injured Servicemen and women, HRH The Duke of Cambridge said: "When Harry and I like so many other young men and women first donned our Help for Heroes wristbands, only six years ago, not even we as Servicemen, could have guessed the scale of the challenges ahead.

"In 2007, the nation was beginning to wake up to the reality of the debt that it owed its wounded and sick Servicemen, returning from Iraq and Afghanistan. The British public's unprecedented response to the likes of Help for Heroes, the Royal British Legion and countless other Service charities was a heartfelt reaction to that sense of debt, felt by countless tens of thousands of people, in fact the whole nation who wanted to show support and gratitude."

One of the biggest challenges for the Charity, and the nation, is to ensure that these brave men and women, who have risked it all in service of our country, have the support they need for life."

Smiles of joy outside St Mary's Hospital, on 23rd July 2013 in Paddington.

BORN TO BE KING

The birth of Prince George Alexander Louis of Cambridge to The Duke and Duchess of Cambridge on July 22nd, 2013 lit up Britain and the Commonwealth. Niagara Falls thundered blue in honour of the new prince. In New Zealand there were similar illuminations. Back in London, a blue and white light display featured a stork revolving around the BT Tower saying, "It's a Boy", while the London Eye shimmered with the Union Flag colours. The bells of Westminster Abbey pealed and there were royal gun salutes fired in Green Park and the Tower of London.

It was an intimate family moment, the second in line to the crown of the United Kingdom was also introducing his one-day-old son, Prince George Alexander Louis of Cambridge and third in line, to the world. The choice of George as the baby's first name reflected royal tradition and history. There have been six Kings named George, the last being Her Majesty's father King George VI. Huge crowds and the massed ranks of the international media, many of whom had camped for weeks outside St Mary's Hospital in Paddington for the first sight of the infant prince, were not disappointed.

The smiles on the faces of The Duke and Duchess, their protective touches and private looks between them, said everything. It was a

The official announcement placed in the forecourt of Buckingham Palace.

The first regal wave from the new prince.

The Prince of Wales and The Duchess of Cornwall – about to meet their grandchild for the first time at the Lindo Wing.

The proud grandparents Michael and Carole Middleton.

Celebrations across London – a view of the London Eye.

royal photo opportunity like no other, marked by informality. The Duke wore an open necked shirt with rolled up sleeves and slacks. Thirty one years ago, his father The Prince of Wales, wore a suit for a similar event. It was all much stiffer in those days and a walkabout among the crowd with a royal baby would have been absolutely out of the question. The new parents exchanged banter with well wishers. Princess Diana's dress on that earlier occasion typified 1980s flowing maternity wear, hiding any suggestion of a lingering bump. The Duchess's choice, a bespoke crepe de chine creation was stylishly modern, yet conservative.

The Duke did most of the talking and jokingly remarked about the overdue birth: "I'll remind him of his tardiness when he's a bit older,"he said. He admitted that his son had "a good pair of lungs on him" and that at 8lbs 6ozs was "quite heavy". The name of the baby was then a big secret, but he can in fact expect to have four different titles during his lifetime. He will eventually become The Prince of Wales, as well as The Duke of Cornwall, before becoming King. Both parents said that it was a "very emotional time". There were inevitably questions about nappy changing. The Duchess spilled the beans about her husband's skills, and at that

Previous Kings

King Edward VII.   King George V.   King Edward VIII.   King George VI.

The world's media jostle to get the best shot.

Town crier Tony Appleton proclaims the royal birth.

Prince William accustoms himself with fatherly duties.

Crowds outside Buckingham Palace.

point The Duke obviously thought it was time to go home. He hoped that the hospital and "you guys", a reference to the media, could "all get back to normal" so he and his wife could "go and look after him". The Duke then fitted a baby seat into his car, like any other father, and the family drove off home to Kensington Palace.

But what is "normal" for a prince of the realm, who is in direct line of descent from Egbert, King of Wessex from 802 and of England 827 to 839, and who is destined to become the 43rd monarch since William the Conqueror. That is, of course, all in the future, and baby Cambridge, bearing in mind the strong constitution of The Queen, the fitness of The Duke of Cambridge, and of his grandfather The Prince of Wales, will not reign for many years.

Close family members applauded the birth and The Queen, who said she was "thrilled", also spoke of how the first born was very special. Later she visited her great grandson at Kensington Palace. The Prince of Wales described his grandson as "marvellous... absolutely wonderful", while The Duchess of Cornwall said she understood how much the birth meant to her husband, saying she thought that he would be a "brilliant" grandfather. She believed the birth was "a wonderfully

uplifting moment for the country". The Duchess's mother, Carole Middleton, described the baby as "absolutely beautiful" and assured the crowd outside the hospital, when she arrived with her husband Michael, that the parents were coping "fabulously". Mrs Middleton is expected to help her daughter care for the new baby when The Duke of Cambridge returns to service with the RAF after his paternity leave.

Life will never be the same again for The Duke and Duchess of Cambridge. On July 22nd, 2013 they wrote a page in the history of the British monarchy.

Future Kings

The Prince of Wales.   The Duke of Cambridge.

The Duchess of Cambridge attends the National Review of Queen's Scouts at Windsor Castle in April 2013.

HER OWN
WOMAN

Four decades and a social revolution have passed since Princess Diana hit the public consciousness. She faced a steep learning curve, but emerged as a skilful public performer. Along the way lessons have been learned and this makes it that much easier for anyone fulfilling a similar role. The Duchess of Cambridge has assets that make her task that much simpler, but has shown no signs of wishing to fit into Diana's shoes. She is indeed true to herself.

Princess Diana in 1981.

Princess Diana confessed that she was "terrified out of her tiny little mind" when, only 20-years-old, she joined the royal round. She was, for instance, in the early stages of her pregnancy with Prince William when she undertook a gruelling three-day tour of Wales. The visit was a great success for the fledgling royal, but reporters noticed that surrounded by a rapturous crowd she would suddenly stop smiling, for no obvious reason, with the purest terror showing in her eyes. Perceptive Welsh women warmed to this vulnerability and said that their dearest wish was to take her home, sit her down on the sofa, ply her with many cups of strong tea, lots of well meaning advice and an aspirin to put her right.

The Duchess of Cambridge, who is 31, appears not to be suffering similar angst in her own transformation from middle class girl

The Duchess of Cambridge at the Diamond Jubilee Pageant in 2012.

The Duchess of Cambridge visits a mosque in Kuala Lumpur in September 2012.

The Duke and Duchess of Cambridge in the South Pacific in 2012.

ASTON MARTIN

We're celebrating our new-born too.

Our warmest wishes to the Royal couple.
From Aston Martin, celebrating a century
of Power, Beauty and Soul.

www.astonmartin.com/100

1913 – 2013

CC100 Speedster Concept

The Prince of Wales and The Duchess and Duke of Cambridge during a visit to Dumfries House in Ayrshire, Scotland in April 2013.

The Duchess of Cambridge in the Solomon Islands, 2012.

The Duchess of Cambridge pays her respects at a war grave cemetary in Singapore, 2012.

The Duchess of Cambridge christens the cruise ship The Royal Princess in June 2013.

ROYAL PRINCESS

Such is the poise and assurance she has displayed since joining the Royal Family – "firm", as Prince Philip calls it – that commentators tend to describe her as "serene, savvy, a natural".

to future Queen Consort. Such is the poise and assurance she has displayed since joining the Royal Family – "firm", as Prince Philip calls it – that commentators tend to describe her as "serene, savvy – a natural". However, she is believed to be wary of comparisons with Princess Diana, although the engagement ring on her finger is an inevitable reminder of someone whose experience of royal life was often less happy. Courtiers past and present dismiss any comparison as invidious, and claim that the differences between them considerably outnumber the similarities. They point to one significant reason: that the two women, when

(above) The Duchess takes to the hockey field during a visit to her old preparatory school, St Andrew's in Pangbourne, 2012.

The Duchess of Cambridge visits the "Expanding Horizons" Primary School Scheme in Kent, 2012.

Prince Harry and The Duke and Duchess of Cambridge wave their wands on the set of the Harry Potter Films at Warner Bros studios in Leavesden, Hertfordshire, April 2013.

SCRIBBULUS

The Duchess of Cambridge chats to children as she visits
Naomi House Children's Hospice near Winchester in 2013.

The Duke and Duchess of Cambridge attend the Irish Guards' St. Patrick's Day Parade in Aldershot, March 2013.

they married were at very different stages of their lives. Princess Diana, they say, had led a very sheltered existence before she was suddenly thrust into the spotlight, while The Duchess was much more worldly wise, better educated, had travelled, and therefore benefited from a personality which was altogether more fully formed.

Insiders say that she is a fast learner, and has shown diligence in researching the causes she wants to support, and the preparation she does before each visit. She is confident and a good listener, a skill enhanced by watching The Queen at close quarters. Those closest to her say the secret of her success is that she is always in the driving seat, in choosing the charities she wants to support, and deciding where or what she would visit. So far she has agreed to be Patron of seven charities, although the eventual plan is for her to have formal links with perhaps 20 or 30 causes at a time. She shares the view of the younger royals that rationing support will have more impact on each cause, and add to its public awareness.

The Duchess has been carrying out solo engagements all over the country – she launched a ship at Southampton on June 13 – but royal duties will have to take second place for at least a while once the third in line to the throne is born. After all every working mother is entitled to maternity leave. Meanwhile The Duke's three-year tour of duty with his RAF Search and Rescue Squadron on Anglesey will end in September. He is said to be considering a new position in the army, a role as adjutant with the Blues and Royals, part of the Household Cavalry, into which he was commissioned in 2006. Much of his time will then be divided between the Household Cavalry Barracks at Windsor and Knightsbridge. In addition he is understood to have agreed to an increase in his official royal duties. The Household Cavalry has strong links with the Royal Family. The Queen is Colonel-in-Chief of the regiment and The Princess Royal is Colonel. The Duke is Colonel of the Irish Guards. 👑

The Duke of Cambridge shows The Queen the ropes during her visit to RAF Valley in 2011.

The Duchess of Cambridge arrives at a reception to celebrate the work of The Art Room charity at The National Portrait Gallery in April 2013.

The beginning of a new era – The Duke and Duchess of Cambridge on the balcony of Buckingham Palace after their marriage in 2011.

FROM PIT TO
PALACE

It must have given The Queen immense satisfaction to have her family gathered around her at the 60th anniversary service commemorating her 1953 Coronation. For despite the spectacle in Westminster Abbey, it was also a very personal occasion, and represented the continuation of the Windsor dynasty – no more so than in the presence of The Duchess of Cambridge, who was about to present Her Majesty with the third in line to the throne.

O nce upon a time it would have beggared belief that a descendant of a miner in the Durham coalfields will one day reign over us. But that is what has happened with the birth of the third in line to the throne of the United Kingdom, and it is the epitome of a desire for betterment in an increasingly meritocratic society, untrammelled by inherited privilege.

The Duchess of Cambridge can rightly be described as "A Princess from the People", as her family tree is almost entirely untouched by aristocracy – although the genealogists have claimed that Prince William and his wife are 17th cousins through a common, if exceedingly torturous, descent from Sir Thomas Fairfax (1612-71), the parliamentary general in the English Civil War, who in 1660 helped to bring about the restoration of the monarchy after the death of Oliver Cromwell.

The astonishing journey from pit to palace began with The Duchess's maternal great-great-great-great grandfather, James Harrison, who worked as a coal miner in the newly-sunk Byers pit in Hetton-le-Hole, Co Durham, in 1821. It would be three generations before his descendants escaped the subterranean life and found a trade above ground. There is a subtle irony here. The richest pit owner in the North East was Sir George Bowes.

Byers pit in Hetton-le-Hole, Co Durham, in 1821.

The Royal Procession leaves Westminister Abbey after the service to mark the 60th anniversary of Her Majesty's Coronation in 2013. It symbolised the line of succession.

The Queen Mother celebrates her 94th birthday outside Clarence House with her great-grandson in 1994.

A pit family. The Duchess's great-grandfather Tom (front left).

His daughter, Mary Eleanor, inherited his wealth, valued in today's money at over £105 million, but the family conscious father added a codicil to his will, stipulating that any future husband of his heiress daughter must adopt his surname, Mary was wooed and won by the impoverished Scottish laird, John Lyon, the 9th Earl of Strathmore, whose family had lost a fortune backing the fiercely Protestant Covenanters in Scotland's interminable wars of religion against English imposed episcopacy. Lord Strathmore had to adopt Bowes-Lyon as his surname. His direct descendant Lady Elizabeth Bowes-Lyon, youngest daughter of the 14th Earl, became the wife of George VI, and was Prince William's great-grandmother. As a young woman, deeply conscious of her Scottish heritage, she preferred to be known as Elizabeth Lyon.

James Harrison spent his life toiling in the pits, as did his son John, and his grandson, also John. But The Duchess's great grandfather, Tom, became a mould-breaker, and found work as an apprentice carpenter, finally settling in Ealing, West London. He was the originator of the family's social ascent.

The Duchess's grandmother, Dorothy, said to be a determined and ambitious girl, married Ronald Goldsmith, a London builder, and by dint of hard work, the couple were able to buy their own house, an unusual achievement for a working class couple in the early 1950s. The Duchess's mother, Carole, was brought up there, in an atmosphere of aspiration, and married Michael Middleton in 1980. It was a fusion of the solid, comfortably off, professional middle class Yorkshire Middleton's, and a working class family who had journeyed in four generations from the coal face in the north-east of England to a modest home-owning family in West London. Their union was also an example of the social revolution that generated by World War I, was consolidated in the aftermath of WWII.

The couple had met while working for British Airways, Michael as a senior flight dispatcher, the man responsible for an aircraft while it is on the ground, and Carole a flight

(above) Carole and Michael Middleton ride in proccession after the marriage of their daughter.

(left) The coal Heiress Mary Eleanor Bowes, Countess of Strathmore and ancestress of The Queen Mother.

18-year-old Prince William poses as a member of Pop, Eton's select group of 21 elected prefects who are allowed to wear a waistcoat of their choice. Pop originated in 1811 as a debating society.

start rite

CARING FOR ROYAL FEET SINCE 1955

LIMITED EDITION

COUNTRY LIFE ®

The essential companion to English country life, providing a
unique and eclectic blend of news and features covering gardens, architecture,
interiors, the Arts, countryside and wildlife, together with magnificent country
houses for sale and matters of cultural significance.

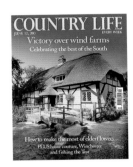

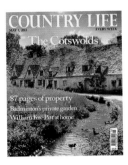

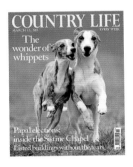

COUNTRY LIFE would like to congratulate The Duke and Duchess
of Cambridge on the wonderful news

Don't miss The Prince of Wales guest editing the November 13 issue

On sale every Wednesday in print and digitally

COUNTRY LIFE.CO.UK

Rock climber Kate.

School days in Pangbourne.

A Middleton family holiday.

Prince William and Kate Middleton on their
graduation day at St Andrew's University in 2005.

Michael and Carole Middleton on the day of the engagement of their daughter to Prince William in 2010.

attendant. Michael's father had been an airline pilot and flying instructor. Before that the family had been prosperous and well connected lawyers in Leeds. Michael Middleton's maternal grandmother, Olive Lupton, was the daughter of a Leeds wool merchant, and she brought a significant dowry to the Middleton family.

Carole Middleton ensured that her own children followed the path of an English middle class family, and at the same time her inbred business flair took wing when she spotted a market among other mothers, at her elder daughter's pre-school play group, for ready-made up bags of sweets and novelties to distribute at their children's parties. When Michael and Carole took the then innovative step of advertising their wares on the internet, the business really took off. Their financial success led to The Duchess's enrolment at Marlborough, the highly regarded public school in Wiltshire founded in 1843 to educate the sons of Church of England clergymen,

subsequently broadening its intake and finally admitting girls in 1968. Its prominent alumni includes the poets Sir John Betjeman and Siegfried Sassoon, the film actor James Mason, the yachtsman Sir Francis Chichester, the pop singer Chris de Burgh, the art historian and Communist spy Anthony Blunt and Samantha Cameron, wife of the Prime Minister. The Duchess flourished there, rubbing shoulders with the children of influential and distinguished parents, giving her a patina of sophistication and self-confidence that would later stand her in good stead.

Her academic qualifications were sufficient for her to gain entrance to St Andrews University, popular among English undergraduates of a certain social standing. It was almost inevitable that she would meet Prince William, whose choice of university had been governed by several factors, some of them political. Given Scotland's progress to devolution and a degree of independence, a Prince studying north of the

The Duchess of Cambridge arrives back at Buckingham Palace in a horse drawn carriage after the Trooping the Colour parade at Horse Guards Parade in June 2013. It was her last official engagement before the birth of her baby.

The couple pose in St. James's Palace just after they announced their engagement in 2010. They stand below the portrait of King William IV.

border would help underpin the monarchy's position there. He considered Edinburgh, but eventually chose the even more ancient institution of St Andrews, not least because of its location on a remote windy corner of North East Fife, which made policing his security somewhat easier than in the heart of the large and cosmopolitan Scottish capital. He was relieved to find that the 16,000 canny citizens of the nearby town tended to leave famous students in their midst well alone, a sensitivity for which he was grateful.

They shared "digs" with student friends, and The Duchess would be seen partnering Prince William at university social events, but the cat finally leapt from the bag when, during their third undergraduate year, they were photographed together on a Swiss skiing holiday. For all the distractions they both left with creditable degrees; Prince William to pursue his preordained career in the armed forces; The Duchess briefly trained as a photographer with the intention of working in the family business and then took a job as an assistant buyer for a retail chain. At the same time she endured a riot of press speculation as to whether her romance with Prince William was on or off, the clearest indication that it was very much "on" came in late 2010, when her parents were invited to join a private shooting party on The Queen's Balmoral Estate.

From the moment the couple announced their engagement on November 16 that year, the then Catherine Middleton's life changed forever; she was no longer a private citizen, but a de facto member of the Royal Family.

The Duchess of Cambridge during her graduation ceremony at St Andrews in 2005. She graduated with a 2:1 in History of Art and Prince William got a 2:1 in Geography.

From the moment the couple announced their engagement on November 16 that year, the then Catherine Middleton's life changed forever; she was no longer a private citizen, but a de facto member of the Royal Family. Under the Great Seal of the Realm The Queen signed an elaborate endorsement which proclaimed, in transcribed calligraphy, her consent to the union of "Our Most Dearly Beloved Grandson Prince William Arthur Philip Louis of Wales, KG. [Knight of the Garter] and Our Trusty and Well-beloved Catherine Elizabeth Middleton".

Prince William and Kate Middleton attend the wedding of their friends, Harry Mead and Rosie Bradford in the village of Northleach, Gloucestershire in 2010.

SOVEREIGN
of TOMORROW

Just married – Prince William drives himself and his wife down
The Mall to make their way to Clarence House in 2011.

The "Instrument of Consent" featured artwork representative of the bridegroom and bride-to-be. There was a gold cipher of the couple's entwined initials beneath The Prince's coronet. A white lily symbolised St Catherine of Siena whose feast day falls on April 29 and with whom The Duchess shares her name. St Catherine was a 14th century philosopher and theologian, and one of the two patron saints of Italy, ranking with St Francis of Assisi. One of a family of 25 children, she believed she had experienced a mystical marriage with Christ, who told her to enter the public life of the world. She did a lot of good, and was also something of a politician and diplomat.

Beneath St Catherine's lily was a Welsh leek surrounded by Prince William's white three-pronged second in line to the throne motif, and a tiny red escallop from the family arms of Princess Diana's family, the Spencers. There was also the red dragon, the heraldic symbol of Wales; the United Kingdom's floral emblems – the rose, thistle and shamrock – and the Garter belt, The Prince's blue and gold Order of the Most Noble Order of the Garter, Britain's oldest order of chivalry, as well as a large gold "E" for Elizabeth.

Prince William had to ask his grandmother's consent to marry because under the Royal Marriages Act 1772, all descendants of George II must obtain the Sovereign's agreement before they wed, otherwise the marriage is invalid. The Act, an arcane piece of Hanoverian legislation is now being replaced by the Succession to the Crown Bill 2012, which ends the principle of male primogeniture, so that the first child of The Duke and Duchess will succeed to the throne regardless of whether it is a girl or boy.

At his engagement "meet the press" briefing, Prince William appeared to have no side, and was savvy enough to address reporters by their first names. He spoke too in the idiomatic style of his generation, almost blokish at times, and there was no sign of the buttoned up vowels of

Prince William and The Duchess of Cambridge travel in the 1902 State Landau along the Processional Route to Buckingham Palace after their wedding service in 2011.

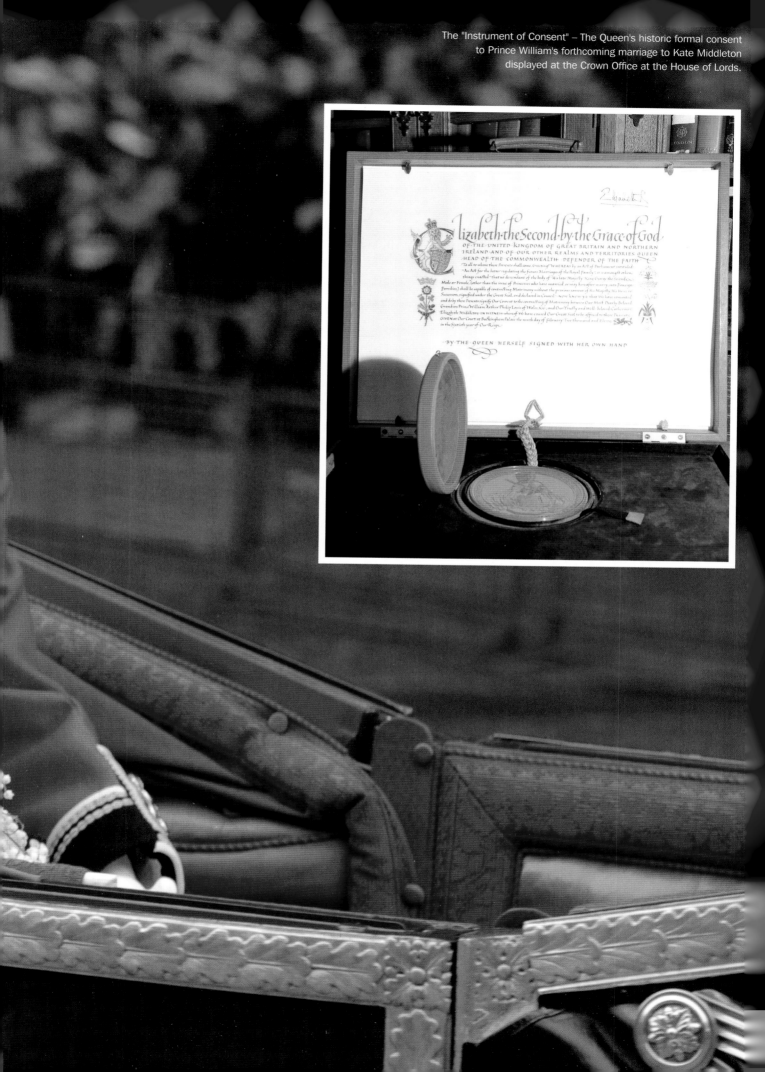

The "Instrument of Consent" – The Queen's historic formal consent to Prince William's forthcoming marriage to Kate Middleton displayed at the Crown Office at the House of Lords.

The Duke and Duchess of Cambridge leave the
King Edward VII Hospital after a routine check-up.

some of the older members of the Royal Family. In choosing his life partner the Prince showed a determination to follow his personal inclinations. The bonus was that in picking a bride from the people he emphasised the point that our monarchy is above and beyond class, and in embodying all classes is representative of us all. The future augers well for his wife, children and for us. The couple's first born will one day be Head of State for 16 nations – 15 of them in the Commonwealth; head of the Armed Forces and Supreme Governor of the Church of England.

But all this is very much in the future. This baby will be unlikely to succeed for half a century or more, after Prince Charles, who has no intention of relinquishing his claim to the throne, and Prince William have had their turn. One has also to bear in mind The Queen's remarkably good health, and the longevity of the late Queen Mother.

The newly minted royal baby will, of course, be surrounded by a certain amount of unavoidable protocol and ceremony, although probably considerably less than its predecessors, but housekeepers, private secretaries, ladies in waiting, and security officers will be the norm for its parents, constant figures in the family home. There will also be nannies, although it is likely that its mother and father will be as hands on as their official duties allow, and, for instance, become adept at nappy changing. But possibly the most radical expectation for their child will be its parents' desire for something rarely afforded to all other royal infants; that it should be raised, and treated, as far as possible, like everyone else's children. Royal Britain, in the wake of Her Majesty's hugely successful Diamond Jubilee is once more riding the crest of the wave. If 2012 was The Queen's year, then 2013 is set to belong to her third great-grandchild.

The Duke and Duchess of Cambridge get in the mood during the 2012 London Olympics.

Prince Charles and Princess Diana with Prince William on his christening in 1982.

ROYAL
CHRISTENINGS

Royal christenings used to be very grand occasions. The baptism of Queen Victoria's eldest daughter was attended by royalty from all over Europe. Her godparents included the King of the Belgians, Queen Adelaide, the widow of King William IV, two royal Duchesses, and one Royal Duke. Today's royal christenings are much more democratic, with godparents drawn not only from royal family members, but personal friends of the parents.

The christening of Victoria, Princess Royal in the Throne Room at Buckingham Palace, 1841. From the picture by C.R. Leslie, R.A.

Christenings in the Royal Family have traditionally been private occasions, attended by family, godparents and close friends. Prince William was, for instance baptised in the Music Room at Buckingham Palace by the Archbishop of Canterbury, Dr Robert Runcie – the same room, as were The Queen's three eldest children, Prince Charles, Princess Anne and The Duke of York. Less grandly, The Duchess of Cambridge was christened as Catherine Elizabeth Middleton at St Andrew's parish church, Bradfield, close to her parents' Berkshire home.

All the royal infants wore the christening robe made in 1841 for the christening of Queen Victoria's eldest daughter, Victoria, The Princess Royal. In 1894 the robe, of fine Honiton lace, lined with white satin was given by The Queen to The Duchess of York, later Queen Mary, the consort of George V, all of whose children wore it. In the next generation it was worn by the daughters of George VI, Princess Elizabeth and Princess Margaret, the two sons of Prince Henry, Duke of Gloucester and the two sons and daughter of Prince George, Duke of Kent. In total over 70 royal babies have been baptised wearing it across 167 years.

Details of the design of the gown are sketchy, but it is believed to have incorporated the same material and lace as formed Queen Victoria's wedding dress. Over the decades the gown has mellowed from the pure white chosen by Victoria to a soft shade of ivory magnolia. It was kept in an airtight container at Buckingham Palace and hand washed in sanitised water between each use, before being lovingly put away until the next royal christening. Our Queen has now retired it, commissioning a replica, first worn in April 2008 by James, Viscount Severn, the son of The Earl and Countess of Wessex.

Prince William's christening in 1982, with members of the Royal Family and his godparents.

Princess Elizabeth holding Prince Charles after his christening in 1948. With her are Queen Mary and King George VI.

Prince William steals the show at the christening of Prince Harry in 1984.

Prince William waves to the crowd as he leaves the Lindo Wing of St. Mary's Hospital, London in 1982, with nanny Barbara Barnes, after visiting his mother and his newborn baby brother, Prince Harry.

ROYAL NANNIES
A LASTING BOND

Until not so very long ago, nannies who were employed in the royal nurseries had no professional training. They were usually young girls from country backgrounds who gained their expertise in looking after children from practical experience as nursery maids in private households. Despite their humble origins, some of them wielded considerable background power. Today trained nannies have tended to be employed to look after royal children.

The Queen and her sister Princess Margaret out for a ride with their nanny Clara Knight in 1933.

Royal children invariably develop an affectionate relationship with their nannies, who sometimes become surrogate mothers, standing in for the biological mothers who are often away on long overseas visits, or touring the country from one end to the other. Despite this call of duty Princess Diana was a constant presence in the lives of her two sons, who knew her simply as "Mummy". One cannot imagine The Duchess of Cambridge being anything but the same.

Princess Diana faced an early test, being obliged to undertake a lengthy official tour to Australia and New Zealand with her husband when Prince William was barely a year old. Eyebrows were raised among the more traditional courtiers when she resolved to take her son with her, encouraged by Malcolm Fraser, the Australian Prime Minister of the time, who thought his countrymen would enjoy the presence of the still-crawling heir but one

Prince Charles on a second birthday outing in St. James's Park with nanny Mabel Anderson.

school it was a good time for her to move on. Prince William never forgot "Baba" and 25 years later he invited her to his wedding.

Two other nannies followed Miss Barnes, but eventually Olga Powell, 60, took over the nursery. She too remained close to Prince William and Prince Harry, even after she retired. She attended Prince Harry's 21st birthday party and his graduation from Sandhurst as well as Prince William's wedding. The week before she died, suddenly, aged 82, in September 2012, she wrote to Prince Harry in Afghanistan, concerned about his safety after a Taliban attack on Camp Bastion where he was stationed as an Apache helicopter pilot.

Prince William cancelled four high profile engagements in the north-east to be at Mrs Powell's funeral in Essex. The enduring relationship between Mrs Powell and Miss Barnes with the Princes was part of a long tradition of carers to royal children continuing to influence their former charges into adulthood.

The days of the infant Prince Charles were supervised by his two nannies, although The Queen still bathed him – when she could.

to the Australian throne. They did, and in their no nonsense way promptly christened him "Billy the Kid".

But William loved his nannies and there was a strong bond between him and Barbara Barnes, a forestry workers daughter who had formerly been nanny to the children of Lord and Lady Glenconner. Miss Barnes had a sense of fun and was devoted to him, sheltering him from much of the fall out from the collapse of his parents' marriage. He called her "Baba", and by all accounts, although he was quite a handful, she was told that she must never smack him or raise her voice if he misbehaved. Her career at Kensington Palace ended when her four-year-old charge started at Wetherby pre-preparatory school in West London. A statement was released saying that The Prince and Princess of Wales, and Miss Barnes, 43, had "mutually agreed" that since Prince William had begun

The Prince of Wales arrives at Aberdeen railway station on his way to the Royal Family's retreat at Balmoral. He took his two sons, six-year-old Prince William, left, and four-year-old Prince Harry, accompanied by their nanny Ruth Wallace.

21st June 1982 – The Prince and Princess of Wales leave the hospital after the birth of Prince William.

Prince Charles in the arms of midwife Helen Maud Rowe after his christening in 1948.

One of the first pictures of Princess Anne walking – with Prince Charles and their nurse Miss Helen Lightbody, at Ballater in 1952.

Prince Andrew walks hand in hand with The Queen and his nanny Mabel Anderson, at Liverpool Street Station, London in 1962.

Princess Margaret with Royal children, left to right, Viscount Linley, Prince Edward, Prince Andrew and Lady Sarah Armstrong-Jones in 1968.

Prince Charles waves to his parents as they pass Clarence House in the Royal Procession for the Festival of Britain. With him is Prince Richard of Gloucester and nannies Ellen Woodburn, left, and Mabel Anderson in 1951.

Helen Lightbody was nanny to both Prince Charles and Princess Anne, until she retired in 1956 to a Duchy of Cornwall apartment in Kennington, South London. She was succeeded by Mabel Anderson, who was a member of the Royal Household for decades, and has been described as one of the most significant influences over The Prince of Wales. Quiet and unassuming she was a figure of continuity in his childhood and maintained a close relationship with the Royal Family long after she ceased to work for them. Prince Charles personally supervised the redecoration of her "Grace and Favour" home in Windsor Home Park, close to the castle. As recently as 2010 Miss Anderson accompanied the Royal Family on a summer cruise round the Western Isles of Scotland to celebrate the 60th birthday of Princess Anne and the 50th birthday of The Duke of York.

For years there was a tradition in the Royal Household to recruit young girls from country backgrounds as nannies. The Queen's nanny was Clara Knight, a farmer's daughter raised on the Hertfordshire estate of the Earl and Countess of Strathmore. She was only 17 when Lady Strathmore chose her as the nursemaid for her baby daughter, Lady Elizabeth Bowes-Lyon, who in turn as Duchess of York, appointed her as nanny for her daughter, Princess Elizabeth. Miss Knight, who was known in the Royal Family by her nickname "Alla" also took care of Princess Margaret from the time she was born. The nursery maid to the two Princesses was Margaret MacDonald, the daughter of a Scottish railway man. Always known to The Queen as "Bobo" Miss MacDonald served her "Little Lady", as she referred to The Queen, for 67 years, becoming Her Majesty's Dresser, palace speak for Ladies Maid, in the 1940s. She was one of the few people completely trusted by The Queen, and her conservative tastes prevailed over her employers' choice of clothes. She would say virtually anything she liked, and The Queen let her get away with it. Miss MacDonald died in 1993, aged 89, in her private suite at Buckingham Palace. The

Four-year-old Prince Harry inspects HMS Belfast with his nanny Ruth Wallace in 1989.

Queen rarely attends funerals, preferring to be represented, but she went to "Bobo's".

The sometimes brisk experience of being looked after by a British nanny was not unique to our Royal Family. Thousands of British girls travelled to Europe and further afield to meet the demand, the consensus being that the best nannies in the world came from the United Kingdom. The wealthy and the fashionable cried out for the British breed, and nowhere was this more true than in the courts and palaces of royalty. Future rulers grew up speaking English as their first language, following the same nursery routines as in Buckingham Palace. Alexandra Eagar an Irish nanny taught English to the four daughters of Nicholas II of Russia, the last Tsar, and the Grand Duchesses developed an Irish accent. She exchanged letters with them until their murder in July 1918, and was haunted by their fate for the rest of her life. As in England the Russian Imperial Family treated their nannies almost as members of their intimate circle.

> *Thousands of British girls travelled to Europe and further afield to meet the demand, the consensus being that the best nannies in the world came from the United Kingdom.*

When Kitty Strutton, a bricklayers daughter from Hackney, East London, who was nanny to Tsar Alexander III and his siblings, died in St Petersburg in 1891, the Tsar and the Grand Dukes walked behind her coffin in the funeral procession through the city. There were great privileges in being a British nanny to foreign royalty, but across Europe they shared the tragedies of their employers – revolutions, wars and assassination – faithful to the end. ♔

Princess Diana with Prince William in New Zealand in 1983.

An ariel view of Kensington Palace. The Duke and Duchess of Cambridge are to live in apartment 1A (circled), the former home of Princess Margaret.

A HOME OR TWO OF
ONE'S OWN

In their living quarters, The Duke and Duchess of Cambridge will have everything which is appropriate to lead an official and a private life. Kensington Palace, on the edge of Kensington Gardens is ideal for bringing up children. Indeed Prince William spent his early years there. Anmer Hall, which sits in the grounds of The Queen's Sandringham Estate, is said to be earmarked for The Duke and Duchess, which will provide a rustic retreat for the busy young couple. They will, of course, have access to other residences.

The new royal baby is to have a grand home in Kensington Palace. It is said that about £1 million will be spent renovating the former apartment of Princess Margaret to match the taste and requirements of The Duke and Duchess of Cambridge. A bonus for The Duchess is the closeness of the shops in the High Street, just down the drive. Apartment 1A – apartment is a misnomer – has four storeys, its own walled garden, and appropriately a nursery. Many of the rooms are still painted in the pink and turquoise colour scheme chosen by Princess Margaret and her husband, Lord Snowdon. Iconic figures in the "Swinging Sixties" they decided the old place, which was in state of decay before they moved in, needed a light touch, in keeping with their image.

Prince Charles and Prince William playing in the garden of Kensington Palace in 1984, just days before his second birthday.

The sunken garden in Kensington Palace.

Princess Diana at her desk in Kensington Palace.

But as well as redecorating, there will be new plumbing, rewiring, and the removal of asbestos. The cost of the renovations will be met from the Royal Family's private fortune and official grants. The apartment, which has been empty since the death of The Queen's sister in 2002, includes a dining room, drawing room, and study, a garden room, and extensive staff quarters. Prince William's first choice had been Apartment 8, Princess Diana's old home, where he and Prince Harry lived from their births until 1998, but he felt there were too many memories there. The apartment is now used as offices for Prince Charles. The Kensington Palace complex has long been the home of members of the Royal Family, and the Cambridge's neighbours will be The Queen's cousins, The Duke of Gloucester and his wife Birgitte, The Duke of Kent and Prince and Princess Michael of Kent.

The Duke and Duchess of Cambridge at present divide their time between the two-bedroom Nottingham Cottage, also in the palace complex, and a rented farmhouse on the Isle of Anglesey in north Wales, where they do

The Kensington Palace complex has long been the home of members of the Royal Family, and the Cambridge's neighbours will be The Queen's cousins, The Duke of Gloucester and his wife Birgitte, The Duke of Kent and Prince and Princess Michael of Kent.

their own cooking and washing. The farm is close to The Duke's posting as an RAF search and rescue pilot. Nottingham Cottage was once the "Grace and Favour" home of Marion "Crawfie" Crawford, governess to the then Princess Elizabeth and her sister, who was cast out of royal circles after she wrote and published

Princess Diana and Prince Charles play with the
young Prince William at Kensington Palace in 1982

The Cupola Room in Kensington Palace, part of the State Apartments.

Past Residents of Kensington Palace

Princess Margaret.

Diana, Princess of Wales.

a sugary account of her life with the Princesses. It has been suggested that Prince Harry might take it over. Insiders call it "Nott Cott".

The Duke of Windsor, Edward VIII before he abdicated, called Kensington Palace "the aunt heap", a nod to its reputation as a home for his hard up female relations; Princess Diana always referred to it as "KP". Originally built as Nottingham House, it was the residence of the Earl of Nottingham, Secretary of State to William III, who bought it in 1689. It became The King's rural retreat, and because of the royal presence was designated as a palace. Apartment 1A adjoins the south front of what the 17th century diarist John Evelyn called "a very sweet villa". It occupies one complete wing of Clock Court, designed for King William by Sir Christopher Wren as the carriage approach to the state entrance. After William and his wife Queen Mary the occupants included George I and George II; Queen (although uncrowned) Caroline, the estranged, and flighty wife of George IV; his brother The Duke of Sussex, and for over 60 years Princess Louise, the fourth daughter of Queen Victoria and Prince Albert, and her husband The Duke of Argyle. It remained Princess Louise's official residence from the 1870s until 1939, the year in which she died, aged ninety-one. Thereafter 1A was left empty and rotting, visited only by the ghosts of its past, until Princess Margaret and Lord Snowdon arrived. They brought up their two children, Lord Linley and Lady Sarah Chatto, there, and now, once again the apartment is to be a family home.

The Duke and Duchess of Cambridge might also be getting a country house. The Queen has applied for planning permission for "a major development" to a mansion on her Sandringham Estate, in Norfolk, and it is widely believed that it has been earmarked for her grandson and his wife. Anmer Hall, in the village of Anmer, three miles east of Sandringham, has been part of the estate since 1898. It is a late Georgian

Anmer Hall.

Princess Louise.

King William III and Queen Mary II.

Queen Anne.

house, and at one time, The Duke and Duchess of Kent and their three children lived there. Prince William is said to have fond memories of the house, from the days when Prince Charles's friend, Hugh van Cutsem rented the property, from 1990 to the year 2000. Prince William and Prince Harry were close to the van Cutsem sons, and were regular visitors. The 10-bedroom house is at present subject to a lease which expires in 2017.

Meanwhile Michael and Carole Middleton are also planning a change of scene – to a manor house with its own share of royal history. Neighbours have revealed that the upwardly mobile couple have bought a Grade II listed Georgian house in Berkshire a few miles from their present home, with seven bedrooms, 18 acres of land, and idyllic views. The royal connection comes from King Henry I, who originally bestowed the land on the monks of Reading Abbey. The Brothers created fishponds in the grounds, three of which still exist. In 1540, following the dissolution of the monasteries Henry VIII granted the site to John Winchcombe, the wealthy son of a wool merchant, who four years later entered Parliament. The house later passed to the Hartley family, who still hold the title of Lord and Lady of the Manor – an honour which is not for sale.

ABOUT HELP FOR HEROES

By Matthew Bowen

Lifelong Support

With an aim of setting up a lifelong support network, Help for Heroes is committed to fund and lead the delivery of four Recovery Centres across the UK, in Catterick, Colchester, Tidworth and Plymouth, forming part of the Defence Recovery Capability – a partnership between Help for Heroes, The Ministry of Defence and The Royal British Legion. The Centres are in place to inspire, enable and support our wounded, injured and sick, and their families, for the rest of their lives. They offer opportunities to retrain for a new career, uncover new passions, or simply find a satisfying hobby.

The Centres, which were officially opened by The Duke of Cambridge and Prince Harry, are already delivering much needed support, and have seen thousands of wounded, injured and sick Service personnel, veterans and their families get the help they need.

The Centres act as a one-stop-shop providing educational courses, counselling, physiotherapy, adaptive sport facilities, psychological, financial and employment support as well as advice on welfare, housing and other issues. Courses provided at the Centres to date have ranged from photography to dog-handling, guitar-making to writing and cooking to gardening. They are also a place that individuals can return to whenever they need support.

A Family of Support

Help for Heroes recognises the need to support families; the parents, partners and children of our heroes, because they play a key role in the recovery of their loved one and they may need help too. From the moment the wounded individual is flown back to the UK to Queen Elizabeth Hospital Birmingham, their family will be able to be at their bedside without the worry of booking hotels and transport to and from the hospital. Help for Heroes has worked in partnership with the QEHB Charity and US Charity, the Fisher House Foundation, to create a Forces and Families Centre on site at QEHB. Fisher House was officially opened by His Royal Highness The Prince of Wales on 21st June 2013. From working with the families of those who have been injured, Help for Heroes knows how important it is for families to be near loved ones during times of distress, when support is so greatly needed. To have injured personnel at different stages of recovery using the house will be so valuable for those at the beginning of their terrifying journey.

Former Royal Marine Andy Grant with his family.

The wife of a wounded Commanding Officer explains how Fisher House will provide a much needed "home away from home" for Service personnel and their families: "I think that

having the use of Fisher House will be of huge benefit to so many families. It is so important to keep families together. It will also be so good not having to rely on transport to get you back and forth, so you can decide when you want to go and visit and when you need a break."

As well as capital build projects which support families, Help for Heroes has Band of Brothers (BoB) and Band of Sisters (BoS) networks which were created to embrace the wounded and their loved ones, and to ensure a channel of communication between the Servicemen and women, their families, and the Charity. The benefits of these networks are considerable and they are flourishing, with an ever increasing membership total of over 3000.

Thanks to the generosity of the public, the BoB and BoS are regularly treated to days out, tickets to events, free product samples and many other gifts. Beyond the fun of the freebies and the goody-bags, there is a dedicated and sympathetic team, ready to tackle any problem, no matter how large or seemingly small.

Alison Richmond, who heads up the Band of Sisters network, has unique personal experience of life as the partner of one of our wounded: "When David was injured, despite the best efforts of the Regimental Welfare Team, I felt very lonely, isolated and frightened. I know how much I would have benefited from speaking with someone who was sharing this experience which is why I am so passionate about the Band of Sisters. I just hope my experience will help others; I want people to know they are not alone. I know first-hand that for our wounded men and women to make a decent recovery, we have to look after the families who are supporting them."

The Latest Prosthetic Technology

World class prosthetic care for our wounded is something that Help for Heroes has been campaigning for since launching in 2007. Working with BLESMA, Help for Heroes

Help for Heroes' Band of Sisters meet at Tedworth House for the weekend.

lobbied the Government to commission the Murrison Report. This made major suggestions for the revision of care given to veterans and since its publication in 2010, Help for Heroes has continued to push and represent the views of the wounded – both serving and veteran.

In February 2013, Health Minister Dr Dan Poulter visited Tedworth House, the Help for Heroes run Recovery Centre, and announced an investment of £11 million to fund nine NHS Centres specialising in prosthesis. These Centres were named after the Murrison Report, to which H4H was a substantial contributor. To complement the NHS Murrison Centres, the MOD has granted a further £6.5 million to provide the wounded with the most technologically advanced prosthetics currently available, including the Genium "bionic" leg. The Genium will improve our injured Servicemen, women and veteran's ability to climb stairs, walk backwards, crouch and kneel and thus dramatically improve quality of life for amputees. With its high weight limit, users can carry or lift heavier loads and the five day battery life brings greater freedom.

The funding will help transform lives, however there is no one-size-fits-all solution and each individual must be given the best prosthetic for them.

Battle Back

Through the Battle Back programme, funded by Help for Heroes, thousands are enjoying a huge range of adaptive sports from skiing to scuba

HELP *for* HEROES
Support For Our Wounded

HRH The Duke of Cambridge and HRH Prince Harry officially open Help for Heroes run Recovery Centres during a visit to Tedworth House in May 2013.

diving, archery to sitting-volleyball. Those who show talent for a particular sport can progress through the programme to an elite level. The 2012 Paralympics saw eight wounded Service personnel take the world stage competing across various disciplines.

Jon-Allan Butterworth lost his left arm when a rocket exploded next to him whilst on tour in Iraq in 2007. It was after taking part in a Help for Heroes bike ride that Jon-Allan's interest in cycling was born. Jon-Allan's talent for cycling saw him represent his country in the London 2012 Paralympics in Track and Road Cycling where he managed to achieve three silver medals. He said: "London 2012 was an incredible experience. The public really got behind me, not only the crowd at the velodrome, but the whole nation. They made my games that bit more memorable. It was an honour and a privilege to represent my country once more. Without the financial grant from Help for Heroes' Quick Reaction Fund and of course, Battle Back, I wouldn't have been able to progress in cycling as quickly as I have done."

Help for Heroes believes that although not everyone will aspire to be a Paralympian, everyone can achieve a personal best.

Last year, 25 heroes took part in the Warrior Games in San Diego. Prince Harry attended the games and met those taking part. A few days later Harry received an award for Distinguished Humanitarian Leadership, and on receiving the award, he referred to the heroes he had met saying: "So many of our Servicemen and women have made the ultimate sacrifice; so many lives have been lost and so many changed forever by the wounds that they have suffered. They have paid a terrible price to keep us safe and free. The

Paralympic cyclist, Jon-Allan Butterworth, holding up one of his three silver medals at London 2012. He first started competitive cycling under the guidance of Help for Heroes.

HELP *for* HEROES
Support For Our Wounded

HRH Prince Harry with the UK team at the Warrior Games during an introduction to Paralympic sports for injured Service members and veterans.

very least we owe them is to make sure that they and their brave families have everything they need through their darkest days – and, in time, regain the hope and confidence to flourish again. For these selfless people, it is after the guns have fallen silent, the din of battle quietened, that the real fight begins – a fight that may last for the rest of their lives."

This year, 34 athletes took part in the games and Prince Harry once again showed his support by meeting them.

Hero Challenges –
The Race Across America

June 2012 saw eight wounded heroes take on one of the world's pre-eminent and longest running endurance cycling events, which is renowned as an extraordinary test for any able bodied competitor.

Every rider in the Help for Heroes Battle Back Team had been either wounded on operations or injured while training for operations, including four double amputees who tackled this phenomenal challenge. During the race, our heroes climbed well over 100,000 feet while passing through 12 states and covering a total distance of 3,051 miles, the difficulty of which is almost unimaginable.

The team completed the race in just seven days, seven hours and 39 minutes with an average speed of over 17mph, exceeding their aim to complete it in eight days with an average speed of just over 15mph.

The team received a huge welcome as they arrived into Annapolis. The cheers were deafening and everyone wanted to come and shake the rider's hands and show their admiration of them completing such an epic challenge. It was a great reminder of the importance of such events to inspire, enable and support our wounded heroes who have given so much.

Row2Recovery

Row2Recovery was developed by three former British Army commanders who trained together at Sandhurst and saw extensive combat in Iraq and Afghanistan.

Tony Harris lost his left leg when an Improvised Explosive Device (IED) detonated under his vehicle in May 2009. Tony and

HELP *for* HEROES

Support For Our Wounded

HRH The Duchess of Cornwall sets off the 2013 Big Battlefield Bike Ride, from Paris to London.

two friends, Ed Janvrin and Alex Mackenzie witnessed friends and comrades sustain life-changing injuries.

At the end of 2011, ex-captains Ed Janvrin and Alex Mackenzie and four other injured Servicemen embarked on an epic 3,000 mile voyage across the Atlantic Ocean in a rowing boat.

The campaign shone a spotlight on the extraordinary achievements of people with disabilities, and challenged misconceptions about what life is like for an injured solider and their family. It also inspired others with life altering injuries to realise their potential.

Money raised was distributed between three key military charities: Help for Heroes, the Soldiers, Sailors, Airmen and Families Association (SSAFA) and ABF – The Soldiers' Charity.

Hero Ride 2013

On Sunday 3 June 2013, over 1,300 cyclists took part in the Help for Heroes Hero Ride. Travelling to Blackheath, London, from all corners of the country, fundraisers were led by over 150 wounded veterans and Service personnel from the UK, USA and Canada for the final ten miles, before crossing the finish line at Horse Guards Parade. Members of the public lined The Mall to support the riders in what was the biggest cycling show of support for our wounded that this country has ever seen.

The ride culminated at Horse Guards Parade with a military celebration including performances from The Games Maker Choir and The State Trumpeters.

Hundreds of organised bike rides took place in the lead up to the finale. The first was the Big Battlefield Bike Ride (BBBR) which

HELP *for* HEROES

Support For Our Wounded

Members of H4H team at the Warrior Games in the US.

saw 300 cyclists ride over 350 miles from Paris to London. The large group of fundraisers were waved off by The Duchess of Cornwall at Les Invalides when they set off on Tuesday 28th May.

Cpl Josh Boggi, a triple amputee who took part in this year's BBBR said: "I wanted to do this ride because Help for Heroes helped me and I wanted to give something back. I've raised £5,000, so if that helps another lad who is where I used to be, then that's good."

In another gallant feat, a team which included 15 wounded Service personnel and veterans cycled 423 miles from Edinburgh into London.

A team of 250 elite cyclists took part in the Dawn Raid Sportive which left the Help for Heroes run Recovery Centre, Tedworth House, in the early hours of Sunday morning. The riders pedalled 90 miles through the night in order to meet with the other cyclists at Blackheath for the final ride into central London.

The atmosphere on Sunday was incredible, with celebrities and the public coming together to show their support for our wounded.

Long time H4H supporter and Patron, Peta Todd, took part in the ride wearing a red Hero Ride shirt. She said:

"We can all be so proud of not only our achievement but also the money that's been raised for Help for Heroes – we are ensuring that their support can continue long-term and our support needs to keep coming!"

Peta's fiancé and Help for Heroes' newest Patron Mark Cavendish, met cyclists at Blackheath and again on Horse Guards Parade.

"The amount of support there was – cars beeping, people clapping – was pretty special. It shows how much people want to get behind our Armed Forces, and what a great charity Help for Heroes is. Some guys have ridden from Paris on hand bikes – it's incredible. To see them and the people supporting them is really moving."

Still Battling

At the royal opening of the Recovery Centres at Tedworth House, The Duke of Cambridge spoke of the need for us to continue supporting our heroes, reflecting the over-arching mission of Help for Heroes. Addressing the gathering which included volunteers, H4H staff, supporters and over 100 injured men and women, His Royal Highness said: "The official opening today of this Recovery Centre does not mark the end of a journey, it marks the beginning. The wounded and sick Servicemen, and their families, who so merit the excellent support that Tedworth House offers, begin lifelong journeys when they arrive here. Journeys into terrain that can be difficult and challenging, but ultimately will be fruitful, thanks to the love and expertise of those who work here and who support this place."

As troops withdraw from Afghanistan in 2014, many will think our work is done, but in truth our work is just beginning. As Bryn Parry says: "They have their whole lives ahead of them and they need us. One day the wars may end, but they will not have peace, they will still be battling and we won't let them battle alone. Thanks to the British public we have a framework of support in place, but we need to keep going. Please help us continue to help our heroes."

Bliss

for babies born too soon,
too small, too sick

DEVOTED TO IMPROVING THE LIVES OF BABIES BORN TOO SOON, TOO SMALL OR TOO SICK

By Jenny Hulme

Behind every charity there is usually the story of one person who inspired a big idea. In this charity's case, it is some very tiny babies – new lives that highlighted a completely unacceptable level of care for premature and poorly newborns in Britain's hospitals. Tiny babies who inspired their families to fight for change for the millions who would follow them into the world too soon, or too small or too sick.

Tiny babies like Arabella Millett. When she was born – five weeks before she was due – she was whisked away from her mother Marie because she was having breathing problems and suffering from a condition that was putting her heart under pressure. In the next agonising 24 hours Marie experienced not only the terrible fear of thinking her daughter would die, but the realisation that the hospital she was in could do little to help her.

"I remember seeing a doctor on the phone in tears as he called one hospital after another searching for an intensive care bed," says Marie.

That was 33 years ago, two years before The Duke and Duchess of Cambridge were born.

It was a time when the medical establishment, and parents on the sharp and heartbreaking end of the problem, were waking up to the fact that the level of care thousands

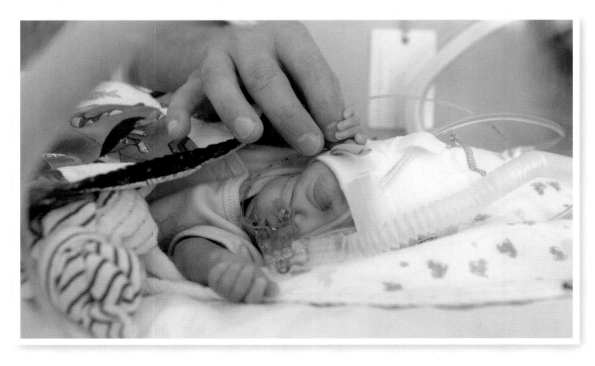

This year more than 80,000 families will call upon Britain's specialist neonatal care services when they have a baby who is born too early (less than 37 weeks into pregnancy), too small (under five and a half pounds) or too sick and in need of life-saving equipment. As you read this, ten newborn babies will be admitted to a special care unit, and ten more will head there every hour. One in four of them will need life saving intensive care.

for babies born too soon,
too small, too sick

...at a time of cut backs

A recent report from Bliss found that neonatal units need more than 1,000 more nurses to provide the right standard of care, yet we are seeing hospital units caring for premature babies cutting staff. In fact one in every eight units are making redundancies or freezing nursing posts when they become vacant. Bliss is at the forefront of a battle to ensure care is not compromised and that a baby's and family's rights are not forgotten.

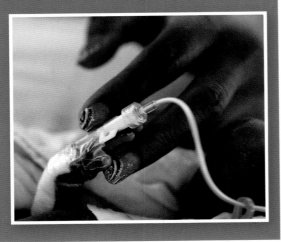

of mothers and babies were receiving was woefully inadequate, and had been for far too long. Thousands of babies were dying as a result, and many more were left with disabilities because they didn't get the care they so badly needed at birth.

But as Marie Millett brought her precious daughter home from hospital, overwhelmed with relief that she had survived, things were about to change. Medical journals started to catalogue the shocking deficiencies and – in 1979 – a national newspaper brought the plight of special care baby units to the attention of the general public. One of its readers, Allan Chilvers, wrote to the newspaper's Letters Page in response, inviting other readers to join him in a Society to help do something about the problem.

That is how Bliss was born and within just a few years they had made 65 hospital

donations, offered three hospital fellowships to fund training, were helping put hundreds of specially trained nurses into the system, and had HRH Duchess of Gloucester as their Patron. More importantly Bliss was matching their extraordinary fundraising efforts with a dogged determination to raise awareness of the issue in the Press and via campaigns and so drive change in the hearts, minds and actions of those making decisions about health policies.

The care of premature and sick babies started, slowly and surely, to become more coordinated. An increasing number of mothers

> "I remember seeing a doctor in tears as he called hospitals searching for an intensive care bed."

and babies were cared for in specialist centres and important medical advances led to an increase in survival rates and improved outcomes.

By 2000 the charity was not only donating millions of pounds worth of equipment, but spending hundreds of thousands on research,

...to end inequality

A baby born in Birmingham is eight times more likely to die than a baby born in Surrey. Bliss continues to campaign for an end to these geographical inequalities and ensure every newborn and its parents have access to the right level of medical care.

Bliss
for babies born too soon,
too small, too sick

nurse training and family support. But it still couldn't keep up with demand, and knew babies were still dying because of a lack of adequate care. So when it donated ten incubators to a London hospital at the start of the new Millennium, the charity ran a campaign to highlight the fact that neonatal units were still – 20 years after its launch – relying on donations. Headlines screamed out about how the NHS were putting babies' lives into the hands of charitable handouts. A few days later the Government announced an additional £6.5 million would be spent on neonatal intensive care.

As with all the best campaigns though, progress only revealed how much more could be achieved. The number of babies born prematurely and sick was increasing every year, and the challenges they faced were becoming ever more complex. Every new innovation or treatment seemed to make an enormous difference, and every new baby seemed to teach the experts something new.

With central funding providing more equipment, Bliss started to divert its resources to professional training and research into innovative long-term projects to improve the care of premature and sick newborns. The charity was invited to join a National Taskforce (made up of doctors, nurses and Department of Health representatives), something they saw as a golden opportunity to raise national standards. In 2005 it created the Bliss Baby Charter based on seven principles setting standards for the care of children.

Central to this is family centred care – a very special package of initiatives that puts the physical, psychological and social needs of both the baby and its family at the heart of the service they receive. Things most new parents take pretty much for granted – the right to hold their baby or feed their baby, the chance to have family and friends close by – had for too long been denied or overlooked in intensive care units. The charity's research, however, was

...to help parents at the hospital

Kangaroo Care – skin-to-skin contact created by placing the newborn on the parent's bare chest – can make a positive difference. Bliss has shown premature and sick babies sleep better, register less pain (for instance when having a blood test), feed better and settle more easily; a baby's heart rate improves and vital signs can become more stable when held close to their parents. Mothers find their milk supply improves making it easier to breast feed, and they feel more confident and relaxed as a result. Crucially it enables parents to bond, something that transforms the experience in intensive care and, when the worst happens, can make a loss more bearable. Bereaved parents tell the charity that Kangaroo Care enabled them to let their baby know they were there, and how much they loved them in their too short a life. Today the charity not only educates nursing staff and parents about the benefits of Kangaroo Care, it works to ensure the logistical problems (working round complex machinery, creating private spaces where it can happen) can be overcome.

2013 the campaign continues...

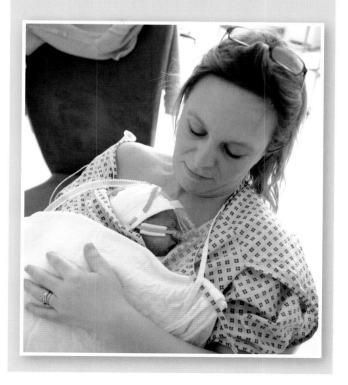

Bliss
for babies born too soon,
too small, too sick

...when a baby goes home

Most parents bring babies home to gifts and balloons and the open arms of grandparents, siblings, friends and neighbours. For many mothers and fathers however, it can mark the end of weeks or months in hospital, when they didn't know from one day, or one hour to the next, or whether their new baby will live or die. Coming home is often a time described as a mix of "extreme happiness and extreme anxiety". New cots and clothes are secondary to oxygen tanks and baskets of medication. Parents may feel adrift from the safety net of support they've had in hospital and health problems are often ongoing. More worryingly, health professionals now overseeing the care of the family may have no experience of pre-term babies and information in parenting magazines or even official health service books may not mention the subject. It's often left to parents to seek out the expert help they need.

Bliss is campaigning for health specialists in the community to have training in the issues of prematurity and have introduced a specialist information programme for community health professionals, including an information guide and study days. The charity also knows mothers of premature babies are especially vulnerable to post-natal depression and so offers free counselling for parents and a training programme for counsellors in the issues surrounding prematurity.

showing that helping mothers breastfeed their baby, or parents hold their baby, giving them emotional support when they were a long way from home and wondering whether their baby would survive the day, could not only help families through this traumatic time, but also improve the health and outcomes of their newborn and reduce the time they needed to spend in a special care baby unit.

Today Bliss is creating a new sort of nursing army to help make that happen. In the last couple of years Bliss Nurses have been recruited in major intensive care centres around the UK. They do not undertake routine nursing tasks, but rather work directly with families – helping to build

By the year 2000 Bliss was donating millions of pounds worth of equipment...

confidence in a parent's ability to look after their baby and to cope with the emotional challenges of having a baby admitted into neonatal care. They are already having an impact on thousands of families each year by ensuring this family centred approach. The charity now has a bold ambition to recruit and fund a Bliss Nurse for every major intensive care unit around the UK (after the first three years the NHS have committed to taking over the funding of these staff). They are aiming for 28 Bliss Nurses by the end of 2020 (with at least the first 12 in post by 2016).

The charity is also determined to fill the gaping hole in information for parents of premature or sick babies (the issue is still rarely mentioned in pregnancy guides and magazines) by creating networks of volunteers to offer support and a free national helpline. It's also developed guides on everything from weaning a premature baby to bringing a newborn home when they're on oxygen, from multiple births of premature babies to financial advice for parents who inevitably need to take extra leave. Tens of

National Trust

Congratulations from the National Trust

The National Trust offers The Duke and Duchess of Cambridge warmest congratulations on the birth of your first child. We wish you and your new baby – destined one day to be our future King or Queen – every happiness in the years to come.

We have been caring for special places since 1895, securing visual beauty, visiting pleasure and vital wildlife habitats, for ever, for everyone. To find out more about visiting, enjoying and protecting these precious special places, call us on 0844 800 1895 or visit www.nationaltrust.org.uk

Bliss
for babies born too soon,
too small, too sick

...when a premature baby goes to school

Starting school is a big day for every child, but each year around 15,000 children who were born prematurely in summer months find the day comes too soon. They are expected to start school according to when they were born (in June, July or August), rather than when they were due (in Autumn).

Bliss recognises this can have an impact on learning and self-esteem, when even the slightest developmental delay can mean children don't start on a level playing field, and may be left struggling to catch up later. Yet parents requests for delayed entry are often refused, leaving some feeling they have little choice but to start their child at school too soon, and others fighting the authorities to have those decisions overturned. Bliss is campaigning for every parent of a premature baby to be able to exercise their right to delay entry until they feel their son or daughter is ready.

thousands of publications have been downloaded, and many more have visited the Bliss website and attended Bliss meetings and seminars.

Nearly 35 years on from its launch there is still so much work Bliss wants to do. Today one in eight babies is born too small, too soon or too sick (that's more than 80,000 each year), and 17,000 need intensive care. At the moment doctors still can't explain one in every three premature births. While advances are saving lives and improving survival rates, the UK still has the highest infant mortality rate in Western Europe and some mothers are, still, transported hundreds of miles simply to find a cot in a unit with the right facilities that can look after them. Bliss believes that is a situation that has to change.

"I am incredibly proud of what Bliss has done in 35 years and the way things have moved forward," says Marie Millet who served as a trustee for Bliss for many years and who, like Carole Middleton, has recently become a grandmother for the first time. Her daughter Arabella gave birth to her own daughter earlier this year.

"I knew when my own grandchild was on the way that the support for babies born prematurely or sick was so much better, but I also knew that new mothers like Arabella can still not be fully guaranteed the care they might need if their baby arrives early or poorly. Can that be possible with all we know now? We're especially horrified that 35 years on, the gap between the best and worst does not seem to be closing," says Marie. "There is still a real shortage of trained nurses, and terrible geographical inequalities. And when you compare the survival rates in this country to the numbers in the rest of Europe, the UK still has one of the worst records. Bliss still has so much to do."

If you would like to find out more about Bliss' current campaigns, or opportunities to volunteer or fundraise, visit bliss.org.uk
Registered charity no. 1002973
Scottish registered charity SC040878